Jurassic Blue

VIOLIN PART

monstrous pieces for the beginner violinist

Caroline Lumsden and **Pam Wedgwood**

with illustrations by **Drew Hillier**

Contents

page 3   **Vicious Velociraptor**

3   **Strong Iguanodon**

5   **Scary, scaly Spinosaurus**

6   **Plesiosaurus lives in the sea**

8   **Fly high, Pterodactyl**

9   **Bony Stegosaurus**

11   **Clever Compsognatus**

12   **Lazy Tyrannosaurus Rex**

14   **Triceratops Rocks**

15   **Dotty Diplodocus**

16   **Jurassic Blue**

FABER _ff_ MUSIC

Foreword

I hope you have as much fun playing these pieces as Pam and I had in the writing of them. Feel free to make these pieces your own by adding second verse words where needed, inventing a new noise on the instrument, or trying out different dynamics. You can even create your own dinosaurs!

Caroline Lumsden

I really enjoyed drawing these pictures for you, but now it's YOUR turn to have fun and let your imagination run … WWWWWILD! So go on, grab some pencils and fill the landscapes with your own imaginary dinosaurs—just as long as you remember to play your violin too!

Drew Hillier

© 2002 by Faber Music Ltd
First published in 2002 by Faber Music Ltd
3 Queen Square London WC1N 3AU
Music processed by MusicSet 2000
Printed in England by Caligraving Ltd
All rights reserved

ISBN 0-571-52159-2

To buy Faber Music publications or to find out about the full range of titles available please contact your local music retailer or Faber Music sales enquiries:

Faber Music Limited, Burnt Mill,
Elizabeth Way, Harlow, CM20 2HX England
Tel: +44 (0)1279 82 89 82   Fax: +44 (0)1279 82 89 83
sales@fabermusic.com   fabermusic.com

Scary, scaly Spinosaurus

1 Clap with words
2 Sing with time names

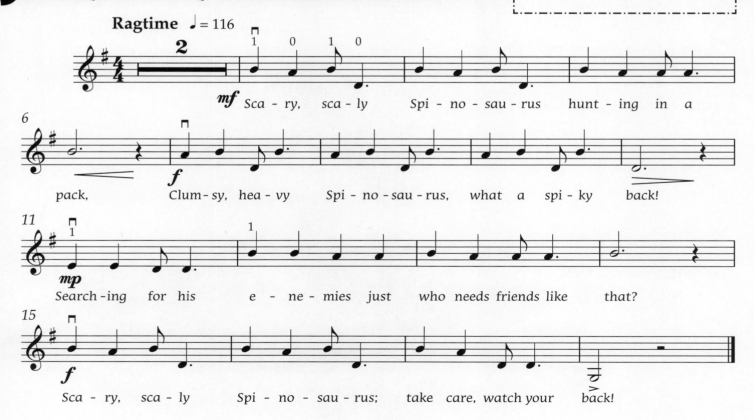

Ragtime ♩ = 116

mf Sca - ry, sca - ly Spi - no - sau - rus hunt - ing in a

pack, *f* Clum - sy, hea - vy Spi - no - sau - rus, what a spi - ky back!

mp Search - ing for his e - ne - mies just who needs friends like that?

f Sca - ry, sca - ly Spi - no - sau - rus; take care, watch your back!

Vicious Velociraptor

1 Clap with words
2 Play

Not too fast: count carefully – you might get eaten! ♩ = 92

Vi - cious Ve - lo - ci - rap - tor,   Vi - cious   Ve - lo - ci -

- rap - tor,   Vi - cious Ve - lo - ci - rap - tor,   vi - cious - ly kills   his

prey.   Yuk!   Grasp - ing the snout and   rip - ping the throat he

kills them with   a   jerk.   Flash - ing his tail   and   gnash - ing his teeth   a

nas - ty piece of   work.   Vi - cious   Ve - lo - ci -

- rap - tor,   you might get   eat - en   for   his   tea!

Which dinosaur is this?

_____

Strong Iguanodon

1 Clap with words
2 Sing with note names

With strength and mystery ♩ = 104

f Strong I - gua - no - don, bold I - gua - no - don,

tear-ing down that huge tree. Strong I - gua - no - don, bold I - gua - no - don,

don't you tan - gle with me. *mf* I - gua - no - don,

I - gua - no - don, *mp* tear - ing down that huge tree.

arco *f* Strong I - gua - no - don, bold I - gua - no - don, spi - ky thumbs, let me be.

ff Strong I - gua - no - don, bold I - gua - no - don, don't you tan - gle with me.

* Think: 4/4 ♩ ♪ ♩ ♪ ♩
slow quick slow quick slow

... and how about this?

Plesiosaurus

on an idea by Alex

1 Play the rhythm 'plesiosaurus' across the D and A strings
2 Learn bars 14–21
3 Play bars 6–13 and 22–end

Sway with the breeze! ♩ = 100

Ple - si - o - sau - rus   lives   in   the sea,   he   u - ses   his   flip - pers

chas - ing   his   tea.   He   twists his   neck   quick - ly   grab - bing   his   prey   and

eats   lit - tle   fish   who   can't   run   a - way!   Glid - ing   si - lent - ly,___

swift - ly   through   the   sea.   'Scrump - tious   lit - tle   fish___

poco rit.   **a tempo**

fol - low   me!'   Ple - si - o - sau - rus   lives   in   the   sea,   he

u - ses   his   flip - pers   chas - ing   his   tea.   He   twists   his   neck   quick - ly

grab - bing   his   prey,   and   eats   lit - tle   fish   who   can't   run   a - way.

Jurassic Blue

VIOLIN and PIANO

monstrous pieces for beginners

Caroline Lumsden and **Pam Wedgwood**

with illustrations by **Drew Hillier**

Contents

score	part	Contents
page 3	3	Scary, scaly Spinosaurus
4	3	Vicious Velociraptor
6	5	Strong Iguanodon
8	6	Plesiosaurus lives in the sea
10	8	Fly high, Pterodactyl
12	9	Bony Stegosaurus
14	11	Clever Compsognatus
16	12	Lazy Tyrannosaurus Rex
18	14	Triceratops Rocks
20	15	Dotty Diplodocus
22	16	Jurassic Blue

© 2002 by Faber Music Ltd
First published in 2002 by Faber Music Ltd
3 Queen Square London WC1N 3AU
Music processed by MusicSet 2000
Printed in England by Caligraving Ltd
All rights reserved

ISBN 0-571-52159-2

To buy Faber Music publications or to find out about
the full range of titles available please contact your
local music retailer or Faber Music sales enquiries:

Faber Music Limited, Burnt Mill, Elizabeth Way, Harlow, CM20 2HX England
Tel: +44 (0)1279 82 89 82   Fax: +44 (0)1279 82 89 83
sales@fabermusic.com   fabermusic.com

FABER **ff** MUSIC

Foreword

Jurassic Blue developed from working with children on the Beauchamp House Easter String Course 2000.

Following on from **Jackaroo**, these pieces start with a revision of the first finger and then introduce second and third fingers, as well as second finger close and first finger back. The addition of words throughout means that all the pieces can be sung through first with the piano, and teaching points and a suggestion box for learning each new piece are given in the score. You may find the following formula a useful way to tackle a new piece:

1 Sing through once with the words

2 Sing and clap with the time names e.g. slow slow quickety slow

3 Sing and clap with note names e.g. DDDDAAAA (preferably showing a sense of pitch with the hands at the same time). Use 'effs' for F♯ and 'beef' for B♭

4 Finally, play!

With all the jazz rhythms found throughout this book, it is always much better to 'feel' them rather then try to be absolutely precise.

Versions of **Jurassic Blue** for viola and cello are also available, so that pupils can enjoy playing together. To give the viola and cello a better range, however, **Bony Stegosaurus** is in a different key from the violin version.

Finally, encourage children to make these pieces their own by adding second verse words where needed, inventing a new noise on the instrument, or trying out different dynamics. Ask them to write their own dinosaur pieces to encourage improvisation—they can even draw these into their part!

I hope you have as much fun playing these pieces as Pam and I did in writing them.

Caroline Lumsden

Teaching points

- Revision of first finger
- Understanding of 'snappy' rhythm
- Simple string crossing

Scary, scaly Spinosaurus

Suggestion box
1 Clap with words
2 Sing with time names

Teaching points
- Understanding of rests
- Up-bow anacrusis

Vicious Velociraptor

Suggestion box 1 Clap with words 2 Play

Not too fast: count carefully – you might get eaten! ♩ = 92

rip - ping the throat he kills them with a jerk.

Flash - ing his tail and gnash - ing his teeth a nas - ty piece of

work. Vi - cious Ve - lo - ci -

- rap - tor you might get eat - en for his tea!

Teaching points

- Placing of second and third finger on D
- Syncopation

Strong Iguanodon

Suggestion box
1 Clap with words
2 Sing with note names

Teaching points

- Placing of second finger on G
- String crossings
- Holding fingers down

Plesiosaurus

on an idea by Alex

Suggestion box

1 Play the rhythm 'plesiosaurus' across the D and A strings
2 Learn bars 14–21
3 Play bars 6–13 and 22–end

Sway with the breeze! ♩ = 100

Ple - si - o - sau - rus lives in the sea, he u - ses his flip - pers chas - ing his tea. He twists his neck quick - ly grab - bing his prey and eats lit - tle fish who can't run a - way! Glid - ing si - lent - ly,___

Fly high, Pterodactyl

Teaching points

- Placing of third finger on A and E strings
- Bow distribution
- Demonstration of (optional) trill

Suggestion box
1 Sing bars 3–19
2 Play bars 20–27

At a steady speed ♩ = 108

Fly high, Pte-ro-dac - tyl, fly high with me, fly high o-ver cliff tops, we'll reach the sea. Fly high, Pte-ro-dac - tyl, with ti-ny feet, let's search for some

Bony Stegosaurus

on an idea by Matthew

Teaching points
- *Preparation of fingers*
- *String crossing with third finger*
- *Col legno and staccato*

Suggestion box 1 Sing and place fingers
2 Play

Spiky! ♩ = 104

Bo - ny Ste - go - sau - rus,

do you think he saw us, is he look - ing at me?

Bo - ny Ste - go - sau - rus, what a di - no - sau - rus,

to Coda

(2. *ff*) don't you think we should

Teaching points

- *Confidence in singing*
- *Second finger close and stretched on A*
- *Slurring in twos or a whole bar*

Clever Compsognatus

Suggestion box

1. Sing
2. Play slowly with slurs in twos
3. Play using a bow to a bar (once learnt)

Bouncy waltz time ♩ = 112

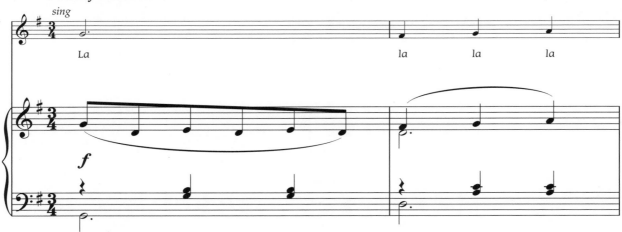

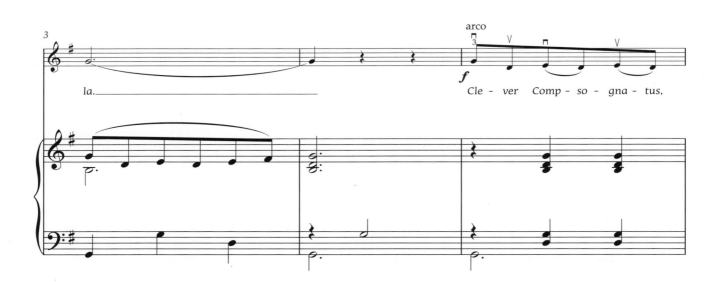

la._____ Cle - ver Comp - so - gna - tus,

dain - ty Comp - so - gna - tus, dart - ing quick - ly, catch - ing prey.

Cle - ver Comp - so - gna - tus, dain - ty Comp - so - gna - tus, don't take fright and run a -

- way. We could both be friends, I'd take you home to tea;

come to stay. Cle - ver Comp - so - gna - tus,

dain - ty comp - so - gna - tus, stay and play.

Teaching points
- $\frac{5}{4}$ time
- Staccato
- Bow distribution

Lazy Tyrannosaurus Rex

Suggestion box
1 Sing
2 Play bars 13–20
3 Play bars 1–12

Relaxed ♩ = 132

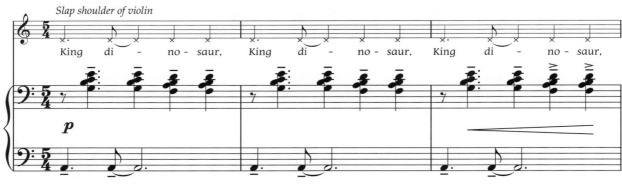

Slap shoulder of violin

King di - no - saur, King di - no - saur, King di - no - saur,

Bouncy

King!

I call the shots round here, I like to shock and scare.

Chal- lenge me if you dare, I'm king. I call the shots round here,

FINE

no- bo- dy dare come near, I am the king di - no - saur.

Triceratops Rocks

on an idea by Phoebe

Teaching points
- Third finger on G
- 'Quicker' rhythm
- Swing elbow

Suggestion box
1 Sing and clap
2 Learn bars 10–13 and 22–25
3 Play

Let's rock 'n' roll ♩ = 116

count 1   2   3   4   1

Tri - ce - ra - tops rocks, yeah,___

Tri - ce - ra - tops rocks, yeah,___   Tri - ce - ra - tops

lock their horns, they love to rock 'n' roll.

pizz. *sing/chant*

Let's rock,   let's rock,   let's rock 'n' roll.

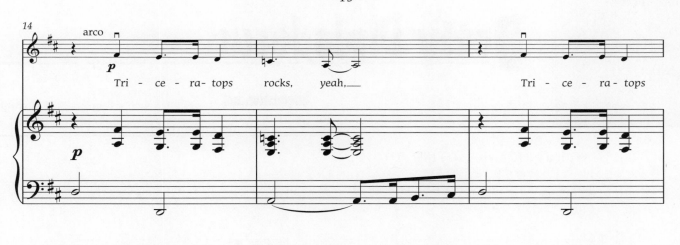

Tri - ce - ra- tops rocks, yeah,___ Tri - ce - ra- tops

rocks, yeah,___ Tri - ce - ra- tops lock their horns, they

love to rock 'n' roll. Let's rock, let's rock,

let's rock 'n' roll, Tri - ce - ra- tops rocks!___

Dotty Diplodocus

Suggestion box

1 Clap bars 5–12 and 20–27
2 Clap bars 14–17
3 Play each section before putting together

With a good swing ♩ = 104 – 116

Dot - ty Dip - lo - do - cus come and dance with me,__ stamp your feet and try to shake your

bo - dy. Dot - ty Dip - lo - do cus come and dance with me,__ hey there,

dance with__ me.__   I'm free.   Come and dance,

Jurassic Blue

Teaching point

- Semitone movement of first and second fingers
- Tap violin with right hand and click with the left

Suggestion box

1 Practise tap and click intro
2 Practise sliding first finger (as bar 5)
3 Have fun playing!

Groovy marcato ♩ = 108

tap click click tap tap tap tap click click tap click click tap tap tap

tap Ju - ras - sic Blue let's groove, Ju - ras - sic Blue let's move, oh come and

join the di - no - saurs, it's cool! Cool to bop and

cool to rave, join the band and show you're brave. Ju - ras - sic

VIOLIN MUSIC FOR THE BEGINNER
FROM FABER MUSIC

Jackaroo

Fantastical pieces for the absolute beginner

CAROLINE LUMSDEN and PAM WEDGWOOD

VIOLIN ISBN 0-571-52149-5
Also available:
VIOLA ISBN 0-571-52169-X
CELLO ISBN 0-571-52189-4

Jurassic Blue

Monstrous pieces for the beginner

CAROLINE LUMSDEN and PAM WEDGWOOD

VIOLIN ISBN 0-571-52159-2
Also available:
VIOLA ISBN 0-571-52179-7
CELLO ISBN 0-571-52199-1

Superstart Level 1

Basic skills and pieces for beginners

MARY COHEN

PUPIL'S BOOK ISBN 0-57151319-0
PIANO ACCOMPANIMENT ISBN 0-571-51711-0

Red Parrot, Green Parrot

*A fresh approach to the
young fiddler's first year*

EDWARD HUWS JONES

PUPIL'S BOOK ISBN 0-571-51171-6
TEACHER'S BOOK ISBN 0-571-51008-6

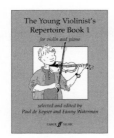

The Young Violinist's Repertoire

*A library of simple classics
for the learner violinist*

PAUL DE KEYSER and FANNY WATERMAN

BOOK 1 ISBN 0-571-50618-6   **BOOK 2** ISBN 0-571-50657-7
BOOK 3 ISBN 0-571-50818-9   **BOOK 4** ISBN 0-571-50819-7

Violin Playtime

Very first pieces with piano accompaniment

PAUL DE KEYSER

BOOK 1 ISBN 0-571-50871-5
BOOK 2 ISBN 0-571-50872-3
BOOK 3 ISBN 0-571-50873-1

FABER *ff* MUSIC

Bony Stegosaurus

on an idea by Matthew

1 Sing and place fingers
2 Play

Spiky! ♩ = 104

Col legno

Bo - ny Ste - go - sau - rus,

do you think he saw us, is he look - ing at me?

to Coda

Bo - ny Ste - go - sau - rus, what a di - no - sau - rus, don't you think we should

flee? Ar - mour pla - ted back - bone, scares your foes a - way.

D. S. al poi al Coda CODA

What an ug - ly crea - ture, turn and run a - way. flee?

Which dinosaur is this?

_____

Clever Compsognatus

1 Sing
2 Play slowly with slurs in twos
3 Play using a bow to a bar
   (once learnt)

Bouncy waltz time ♩ = 112

La   la   la   la   la.

Cle - ver Comp - so - gna - tus, dain - ty Comp - so - gna - tus, dart - ing quick - ly, catch -ing

prey.   Cle - ver Comp - so - gna - tus, dain - ty Comp - so - gna - tus,

don't take fright and run a - way.   We could both be friends, I'd

take you home to tea; come to stay.   Cle - ver Comp - so - gna - tus,

dain - ty comp - so - gna - tus, stay and play.

Lazy Tyrannosaurus Rex

1 Sing
2 Play bars 13–20
3 Play bars 1–12

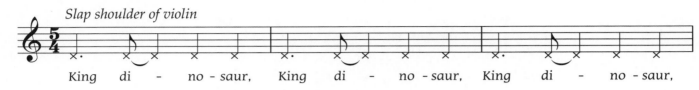

Relaxed ♩ = 132

Slap shoulder of violin

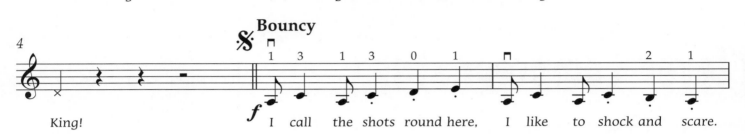

King di - no - saur, King di - no - saur, King di - no - saur,

King! I call the shots round here, I like to shock and scare.

Chal-lenge me if you dare, I'm king. I call the shots round here,

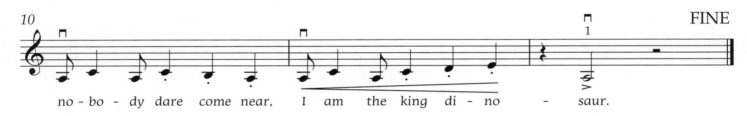

no - bo - dy dare come near, I am the king di - no - saur.

Sleepily

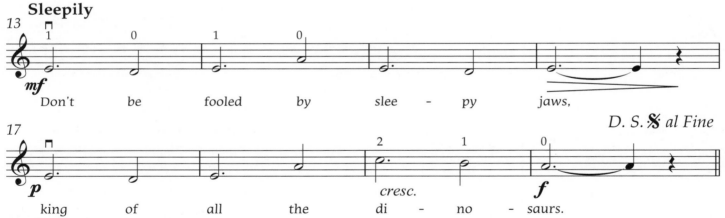

Don't be fooled by slee - py jaws,

D. S. 𝄋 al Fine

king of all the di - no - saurs.

cresc.

Now try inventing your own dinosaur piece!

Triceratops Rocks

on an idea by Phoebe

1 Sing and clap
2 Learn bars 10–13 and 22–25
3 Play

With a good swing ♩ = 104 – 116

finger-click

Dot - ty Dip - lo - do - cus come and dance with me,_ stamp your feet and try to shake your bo - dy. Dot - ty Dip - lo - do - cus come and dance with me,_ hey there,_ dance with_ me._ I'm free.

Come and dance, come and dance, part -ner me,_ part -ner me. dance with me, hey! Dot - ty Dip - lo - do - cus come and dance with me,

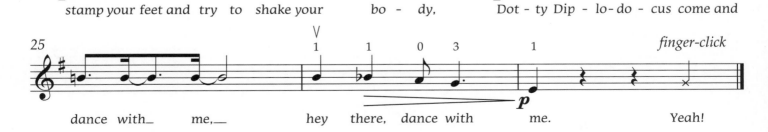

stamp your feet and try to shake your bo - dy, Dot - ty Dip - lo - do - cus come and dance with_ me,_ hey there, dance with me. Yeah!

Dotty Diplodocus

1 Clap bars 5–12 and 20–27
2 Clap bars 14–17
3 Play each section before putting
together

Jurassic Blue

1 Practise tap and click intro
2 Practise sliding first finger
   (as bar 5)
3 Have fun playing!

Groovy marcato ♩ = 108

tap   click   click   tap tap tap   tap   click   click   tap   click   click   tap tap tap

tap   Ju-ras-sic Blue   let's groove,   Ju-ras-sic Blue   let's move,   oh come and

join   the   di - no - saurs,   it's   cool!   Cool   to   bop   and

cool   to   rave,   join   the   band   and   show you're   brave.   Ju-ras-sic

Blue   let's   groove,   Ju-ras-sic Blue   let's   move,   do come and   dance with   di - no -

-saurs,   it's   cool!   Cool   to   bop   and   cool   to   rave,

bring   your   friends be   ve - ry   brave!   Ju-ras-sic Blue   let's   groove,   Ju-ras-sic

Blue   let's   move,   oh won't you   dance all   night   with   Di - no - saurs!